WHAT ARCTIC ANIMALS EAT

This is a polar bear.

It eats seals.

This is a caribou.

It eats lichens.

This is a snowy owl.

It eats lemmings.

This is a narwhal.

It eats fish.

This is a walrus.

It eats clams.

This is a ptarmigan.

It eats plants.

This is a bowhead whale.

It eats crustaceans.